To Rhian Holland

SAGITTARIUS

A guide to living your best astrological life

STELLA ANDROMEDA

ILLUSTRATED BY EVI O. STUDIO

Hardie Grant

BOOKS

Introduction 7

I.

Get to Know Sagittarius

II.

The Sagittarius Deep Dive

III.

Give Me More

Introduction

Inscribed on the forecourt of the ancient Greek temple of Apollo at Delphi are the words 'know thyself'. This is one of the 147 Delphic maxims, or rules to live by, attributed to Apollo himself, and was later extended by the philosopher Socrates to the sentence, 'The unexamined life is not worth living.'

People seek a variety of ways of knowing themselves, of coming to terms with life and trying to find ways to understand the challenges of human existence, often through therapy or belief systems like organised religion. These are ways in which we strive to understand the relationships we have with ourselves and others better, seeking out particular tools that enable us to do so.

As far as systems of understanding human nature and experience go, astrology has much to offer through its symbolic use of the constellations of the heavens, the depictions of the zodiac signs, the planets and their energetic effects. Many people find accessing this information and harnessing its potential a useful way of thinking about how to manage their lives more effectively.

What is astrology?

In simple terms, astrology is the study and interpretation of how the planets can influence us, and the world in which we live, through an understanding of their positions at a specific place in time. The practice of astrology relies on a combination of factual knowledge of the characteristics of these positions and their psychological interpretation.

Astrology is less of a belief system and more of a tool for living, from which ancient and established wisdom can be drawn. Any of us can learn to use astrology, not so much for divination or telling the future, but as a guidebook that provides greater insight and a more thoughtful way of approaching life. Timing is very much at the heart of astrology, and knowledge of planetary configurations and their relationship to each other at specific moments in time can assist in helping us with the timing of some of our life choices and decisions.

Knowing when major life shifts can occur – because of particular planetary configurations such as a Saturn return (see page 103) or Mercury retrograde (see page 104) – or what it means to have Venus in your seventh house (see pages 85 and 98), while recognising the specific characteristics of your sign, are all tools that you can use to your advantage. Knowledge is power, and astrology can be a very powerful supplement to approaching life's ups and downs and any relationships we form along the way.

The 12 signs of the zodiac

Each sign of the zodiac has a range of recognisable characteristics, shared by people born under that sign. This is your Sun sign, which you probably already know – and the usual starting point from which we each begin to explore our own astrological paths. Sun sign characteristics can be strongly exhibited in an individual's make-up; however, this is only part of the picture.

Usually, how we appear to others is tempered by the influence of other factors – and these are worth bearing in mind. Your ascendant sign is equally important, as is the positioning of your Moon. You can also look to your opposite sign to see what your Sun sign may need a little more of, to balance its characteristics.

After getting to know your Sun sign in the first part of this book, you might want to dive into the Give Me More section (see pages 74–105) to start to explore all the particulars of your birth chart. These will give you far greater insight into the myriad astrological influences that may play out in your life.

Sun signs

It takes 365 (and a quarter, to be precise) days for the Earth to orbit the Sun and in so doing, the Sun appears to us to spend a month travelling through each sign of the zodiac. Your Sun sign is therefore an indication of the sign that the Sun was travelling through at the time of your birth. Knowing what Sun signs you and your family, friends and lovers are provides you with just the beginning of the insights into character and personality that astrology can help you discover.

On the cusp

For those for whom a birthday falls close to the end of one Sun sign and the beginning of another, it's worth knowing what time you were born. There's no such thing, astrologically, as being 'on the cusp' – because the signs begin at a specific time on a specific date, although this can vary a little year on year. If you are not sure, you'll need to know your birth date, birth time and birth place to work out accurately to which Sun sign you belong. Once you have these, you can consult an astrologer or run your details through an online astrology site program (see page 108) to give you the most accurate birth chart possible.

Taurus

The bull

★

21 APRIL–20 MAY

Aries

The ram

★

21 MARCH–20 APRIL

Astrologically the first sign of the zodiac, Aries appears alongside the vernal (or spring) equinox. A cardinal fire sign, depicted by the ram, it is the sign of beginnings and ruled by planet Mars, which represents a dynamic ability to meet challenges energetically and creatively. Its opposite sign is airy Libra.

Grounded, sensual and appreciative of bodily pleasures, Taurus is a fixed earth sign endowed by its ruling planet Venus with grace and a love of beauty, despite its depiction as a bull. Generally characterised by an easy and uncomplicated, if occasionally stubborn, approach to life, Taurus' opposite sign is watery Scorpio.

Gemini

The twins

✴

21 MAY–20 JUNE

A mutable air sign symbolised by the twins, Gemini tends to see both sides of an argument, its speedy intellect influenced by its ruling planet Mercury. Tending to fight shy of commitment, this sign also epitomises a certain youthfulness of attitude. Its opposite sign is fiery Sagittarius.

Cancer

The crab

✴

21 JUNE–21 JULY

Depicted by the crab and the tenacity of its claws, Cancer is a cardinal water sign, emotional and intuitive, its sensitivity protected by its shell. Ruled by the maternal Moon, the shell also represents the security of home, to which Cancer is committed. Its opposite sign is earthy Capricorn.

Leo

The lion

★

22 JULY–21 AUGUST

A fixed fire sign, ruled by the Sun, Leo loves to shine and is an idealist at heart, positive and generous to a fault. Depicted by the lion, Leo can roar with pride and be confident and uncompromising, with a great faith and trust in humanity. Its opposite sign is airy Aquarius.

Virgo

The virgin

★

22 AUGUST–21 SEPTEMBER

Traditionally represented as a maiden or virgin, this mutable earth sign is observant, detail oriented and tends towards self-sufficiency. Ruled by Mercury, Virgo benefits from a sharp intellect that can be self-critical, while often being very health conscious. Its opposite sign is watery Pisces.

Scorpio

The scorpion

★

22 OCTOBER–21 NOVEMBER

Given to intense feelings, as befits a fixed water sign, Scorpio is depicted by the scorpion – linking it to the rebirth that follows death – and is ruled by both Pluto and Mars. With a strong spirituality and deep emotions, Scorpio needs security to transform its strength. Its opposite sign is earthy Taurus.

Libra

The scales

★

22 SEPTEMBER–21 OCTOBER

A cardinal air sign, ruled by Venus, Libra is all about beauty, balance (as depicted by the scales) and harmony in its rather romanticised, ideal world. With a strong aesthetic sense, Libra can be both arty and crafty, but also likes fairness and can be very diplomatic. Its opposite sign is fiery Aries.

Sagittarius

The archer

★

22 NOVEMBER–21 DECEMBER

Depicted by the archer, Sagittarius is a mutable fire sign that's all about travel and adventure, in body or mind, and is very direct in approach. Ruled by the benevolent Jupiter, Sagittarius is optimistic with lots of ideas; liking a free rein, but with a tendency to generalise. Its opposite sign is airy Gemini.

Capricorn

The goat

★

22 DECEMBER–20 JANUARY

Ruled by Saturn, Capricorn is a cardinal earth sign associated with hard work and depicted by the sure-footed and sometimes playful goat. Trustworthy and unafraid of commitment, Capricorn is often very self-sufficient and has the discipline for the freelance working life. Its opposite sign is the watery Cancer.

Pisces

The fish

⭐

Acutely responsive to its surroundings, Pisces is a mutable water sign depicted by two fish, swimming in opposite directions, sometimes confusing fantasy with reality. Ruled by Neptune, its world is fluid, imaginative and empathetic, often picking up on the moods of others. Its opposite sign is earthy Virgo.

Aquarius

The water carrier

⭐

21 JANUARY–19 FEBRUARY

Confusingly, given its depiction by the water carrier, Aquarius is a fixed air sign ruled by the unpredictable Uranus, sweeping away old ideas with innovative thinking. Tolerant, open-minded and all about humanity, its vision is social with a conscience. Its opposite sign is fiery Leo.

Know

Sagittarius

The sign the Sun
was travelling in at the
time you were born is the
ultimate starting point
in exploring your character
and personality through
the zodiac.

Mutable fire sign, depicted by the archer and also as a centaur (half man half horse).

Ruled by Jupiter, ruler of the heavens, associated with good fortune and abundance.

OPPOSITE SIGN

Gemini

STATEMENT OF SELF

'I see.'

Lucky colour

Given its status as heavenly ruler, purple, the colour of royalty, is Sagittarius' lucky colour. Wear hues of purple, deep or pale-toned like lavender, when you need a psychological boost and additional courage. If you don't want to be ostentatious with a strong colour, choose purple for accessories – shoes, gloves, socks, hat or underwear.

Lucky day

Thursday is Sagittarius' lucky day, named after Jupiter – in French it's *jeudi,* Italian *giovedi* and Spanish *jueves,* all in acknowledgement of this Roman god. There's also a link to the god of thunder Thor, as Jupiter has a similar role in ruling the heavens.

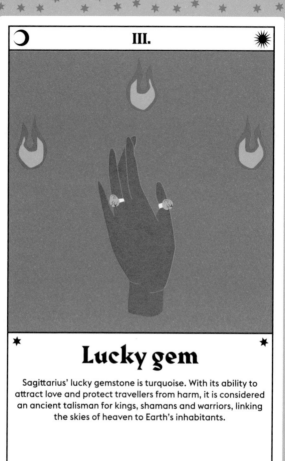

Lucky gem

Sagittarius' lucky gemstone is turquoise. With its ability to attract love and protect travellers from harm, it is considered an ancient talisman for kings, shamans and warriors, linking the skies of heaven to Earth's inhabitants.

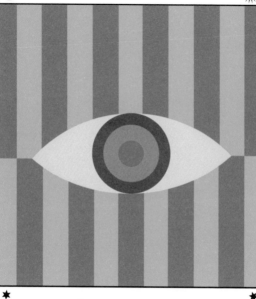

Locations

Home of huge distances, Australia resonates with Sagittarius'
urge for far-flung vistas, as does Spain, the home of ancient
conquistadors and modern travellers, and Hungary is also
a destination for the archer. Cities include Acapulco,
Stuttgart, Naples and Nottingham.

✦
Holidays
✦

Anywhere a horse can run free will attract Sagittarius, both literally and metaphorically, so destinations like trekking in the Drakensberg mountains of South Africa, hiking in the Lake District of the UK or the American Pacific Crest Trail might appeal, as a comatose beach holiday probably won't unless there are spurts of activity in between.

✦   ✦

Flowers

The humble dandelion, which depicts the shining Sun, is one of Sagittarius' flowers, while the golden-headed daffodil is another.

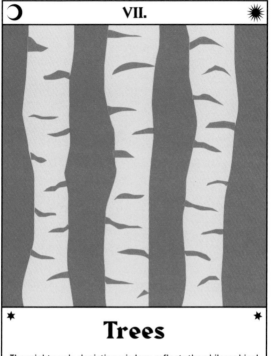

VII.

Trees

The mighty oak, depicting wisdom, reflects the philosophical side of Sagittarius. The birch tree is also a symbol of ancient wisdom while appearing forever young.

Pets

For Sagittarius, the horse is their ideal pet, if not in actuality then in their dreams. Even if they can't own one, there may be an affinity in learning to ride.

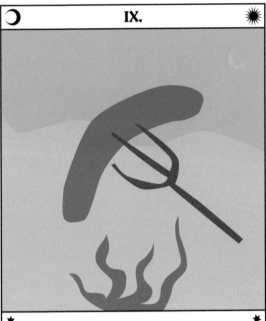

Parties

Happy to travel to party, Sagittarius will be the first to take a flight just for a 24-hour rave before taking the red-eye back to the office. That said, when it comes to planning their own party, it's likely to be a last-minute barbecue because the weather is right, rather than an elegant event six months in the planning. When it comes to a cocktail with an equine kick, there may well be ginger at its heart, as in a bourbon-based Old Fashioned.

Sagittarius characteristics

Sagittarius is all about independence of mind, body and spirit, and this lies at the heart of their approach to life, and a very positive approach it is, too. Positivity radiates from them because in Sagittarius' world, anything and everything is possible: they are seriously optimistic about life's possibilities and somehow this seems to open doors for them, not least because their positivity is hard to resist.

All this makes them very attractive to be around, but the downside is that they may not be around for long. This independence of spirit can make Sagittarius very restless, always in pursuit of new ideas, places and people. Along with this independence is a curiosity and a desire for wisdom. Those arrows fired by the archer into the air? They also represent the pursuit for higher knowledge.

Essentially, Sagittarius is the sign of the explorer and

philosopher and will fire those metaphorical ideas from their bow, then rush off to see where they land, making them an interesting mix of animal instinct and enlightened thinking. Anything can spark the fire of their intellectual curiosity. That pot of gold at the rainbow's end? The minute that rainbow appears, Sagittarius is already out the door trying to find out whether that pot of gold really exists – at least metaphorically speaking.

While Sagittarius may be such good company, kind and jovial, they are sometimes so gregarious it can be hard to keep up. Sagittarius isn't superficial, but the only chance of grabbing their attention probably comes from being seen – out of sight can mean out of mind – and while they are capable of picking up a friendship where they left off, others may not find it so easy. This perplexes Sagittarius as they have no wish to hurt anyone's feelings. But they won't dwell on this thought for long – as they are already onto the next big thing.

All this happy-go-lucky attitude that is Sagittarius' style can mean others sometimes have to pick up the pieces as they chase off after another grand plan, leaving unfinished work, missed deadlines and forgotten appointments lying in their wake. The never-apologise, never-explain attitude can sometimes irk more conscientious types, but the relentless enthusiasm and willingness to make amends can soften the hardest hearts. Along the way, though, they do learn some aspects of responsibility, and Sagittarius is often the first to volunteer to help or do a favour for a friend. Sheer big-heartedness means they will seldom let their friends down – as long as they're not temporarily distracted by something else!

TEMPERING THE FIRE

The key characteristics of any Sun sign can be balanced out (or sometimes reinforced) by the characteristics of other signs in the same birth chart, particularly those of the ascendant and the Moon. So if someone doesn't appear to be typical of their Sun sign, that's why. However, those nascent Sagittarius aspects will always be there as a key influence, informing an individual's approach to life.

Physical Sagittarius

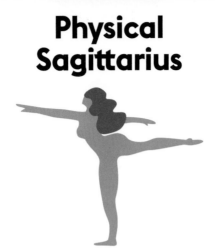

All that robust energy makes Sagittarius one of the most active signs of the zodiac, and they tend to bound into a room, busily looking around for the action, happy to carry others along on the tide of their current enthusiasm. Even when they are physically still, their minds are busy exploring and their restless eyes may be an indication of this. All this internal activity is intent on finding external expression and this can sometimes make Sagittarius a little physically clumsy. There's often something slightly exaggerated about Sagittarius' style, too, and their clothes may be bold and flamboyant, their general appearance very attractive – all of which makes them difficult to miss.

Health

Represented by the half-horse, half-human centaur, it's Sagittarius' legs that can cause problems, particularly the hips and thighs (and sometimes the knees), which take the brunt of all that bounding about. For such a physically strong sign, Sagittarius can be accident prone. The other area of weakness can be in the liver, and any excess in rich foods or alcohol may show up problems there. With a little thought and some of that Sagittarius wisdom, problems can be avoided. Generally, though, Sagittarius isn't the sign of a worrier, and most health problems tend towards the physical rather than the psychological.

Exercise

Naturally inclined toward activity if not formal exercise, which can be a bit of a hit-or-miss affair for Sagittarius, specific exercises that strengthen the muscles to support the joints will help keep problems with hips and legs at bay. Running often appeals, but this can take its toll on the joints, so should be balanced with something like Pilates or yoga. Many are also attracted to horse riding, happy in the saddle where they can literally feel at one with their Sun sign.

How Sagittarius communicates

Extrovert and enthusiastic, Sagittarius is always keen to share ideas and will debate and develop and expand on these as they talk, roaming back and forth and often at high speed. There's lots of gesticulation and even acting out their stories – which can sometimes make their ideas difficult to follow. No matter, as they are probably on to the next thing before you've caught up. They do listen, but only really if what's being said is of specific interest and then they are all ears, like an alert horse. Sagittarius also has a tendency towards tactlessness, not because they are deliberately thoughtless, just sometimes a little clumsy in their responses; but their genuine kind-heartedness means they will promptly apologise if they see they've inadvertently hurt someone's feelings. Pausing to engage their brain before opening their mouth is a lesson some Sagittarians could do well to learn.

Sagittarius careers

Given their enthusiasm and outgoing nature, any public-facing career works well for Sagittarius and particularly in media fields like publicity, advertising, sales or marketing. With a flair for versatility, they can pick up and run with diverse ideas, often coming up with highly creative solutions or formulating innovative ways to promote ideas that really catch the zeitgeist. All well and good, but Sagittarius is often more of an ideas rather than an delivery person; they need to recognise this and learn to delegate or work closely with a team to achieve the best results.

Imagination is strong in Sagittarius, so many of the creative industries attract, whether that is writing, painting, acting or film-making, because of their love for communicating ideas. Teaching, too, where inspiring others' minds and passing on a love of ideas and learning is key, is a great focus for the Sagittarius talent for communication. In the same way, coaching in sports or some other field – life coaching or fitness coaching – suits Sagittarius' ability to link body and mind. Finally, all that wanderlust might find a relevant career in the travel industry, as an agent or a travel writer, exploring and expanding other people's horizons and minds.

How Sagittarius chimes

From lovers to friends, when it comes to other signs, how does Sagittarius get along? Knowledge of other signs and how they interact can be helpful when negotiating relationships, revealed through an understanding of Sun sign characteristics that might chime or chafe. Understanding these through an astrological framework can be really helpful as it can depersonalise potential frictions, taking the sting out of what appears to be in opposition.

Harmonising relationships can sometimes be tricky for freedom-loving Sagittarius, who often takes off at the sign of too much intensity, but how they chime is partly dependent on what other planetary influences are at play in their personal birth chart, toning down or enhancing aspects of their Sun sign characteristics, especially those that can sometimes clash with other signs.

The Sagittarius woman

The Sagittarius woman may be immediately noticeable by the way she tosses her head and seems to flare her nostrils, sniffing new adventures and trotting off, a trail of admirers in her wake. A natural flirt and oblivious to her effect, a partner's best bet is to travel alongside until she can't live without them.

NOTABLE SAGITTARIUS WOMEN

Even Jane Austen travelled through her writing into the minds of others, while French singer Edith Piaf communicated in song. Miley Cyrus and Taylor Swift both show the independence of spirit in careers that provoke admiration, while those free-spirited Sagittarius women Jane Fonda, Bette Midler and Judi Dench led the way.

The Sagittarius man

Sociable by nature, this is a man with a lot of friends who is often out with his mates, playing team sports, down the pub or generally hanging out and shooting the breeze. Anyone interested had better be aware of this and find a way onto his team, as it's often the way he keeps those who love him at arm's length.

Jimi Hendrix, Jamie Foxx, Frank Sinatra and Brad Pitt have all shown a diverse and independent streak which, along with their charm, characterises Sagittarius. Exploring their careers comes as easily as exploring relationships to these freewheeling men, giving them something of a fickle reputation.

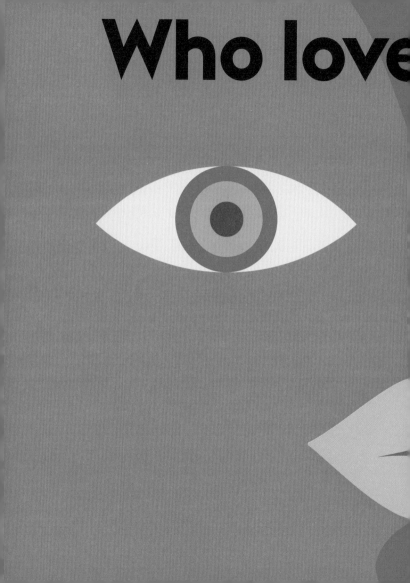

Sagittarius & Aries

Intellectually, physically and with a wide range of shared interests, these two are well suited in numerous ways. Sagittarius' more philosophical approach can sometimes irritate Aries and they both have strong views and tempers – but the sex is hot, too!

Sagittarius & Taurus

Taurus has a need to organise and control that won't sit comfortably with Sagittarius, although the bull's earthy nature can initially attract. In the long term, Sagittarius needs variety, independence and spontaneous fun, which might derail this pairing.

Sagittarius & Gemini

There's a spark of immediate recognition between these two, who share a bright wit and imaginative approach to life and love, proving to be lots of fun both in and out of the bedroom. Even if it doesn't last, it'll be good while it did and amicable on parting.

Sagittarius & Cancer

Sagittarius' freestyle approach to love plays havoc with Cancer's need for security, although the sensuality of the crab is initially intriguing. It's not enough, though, to compensate and keep each other interested, but a friendship could endure.

Sagittarius & Leo

Lots to chime here: with an equal love of adventure, socialising and freedom, there's little conflict about how to spend their time, while Sagittarius' light-hearted approach doesn't clash with Leo's tendency to be rather grand. Happy times.

Sagittarius & Virgo

Lots of interesting conversations to be had on a cerebral level but not much else, and overall Sagittarius tends to find Virgo's need for organisation and attention to detail creates too small a canvas for their freewheeling taste.

Sagittarius & Scorpio

Possessive, intense Scorpio may intrigue Sagittarius and seduce them physically at first, but it's all a bit much and it won't be long before Sagittarius' instinct to run away from the endless confrontations kicks in. Tricky from the word go.

Sagittarius & Libra

There's an unexpected harmony between these two, because Libra adapts easily to Sagittarius' need to explore and offers luxurious opportunities in which to do so, while also balancing an emotional need for freedom.

Sagittarius & Sagittarius

The connection between two like signs can bring out the best in each other – or the worst. While a love of freedom is all very well, they do need to be travelling in the same direction to even get to first base, so may end up more like siblings than soul mates.

Sagittarius & Aquarius

Prospects for this pair are good because they each have a highly imaginative, creative and outgoing side, and won't try to tie each other down. Commitment might take a while because of this and they may be friends first, but the slow burn can be a real turn on.

Sagittarius & Pisces

That fiery energy is very attractive to dreamy Pisces, who finds Sagittarius' wildly exploratory nature exciting. In the end, however, Sagittarius finds all that emotion too restrictive and can come to resent the drain on their freedom.

Sagittarius & Capricorn

Sagittarius' compulsively social side is a mystery to Capricorn, who's a bit of a loner and certainly expects a committed relationship from the word go. Both have high expectations, but these tend to play out too differently to be very compatible.

Sagittarius love-o-meter

Least compatible

Scorpio   Capricorn   Cancer   Pisces   Taurus   Virgo

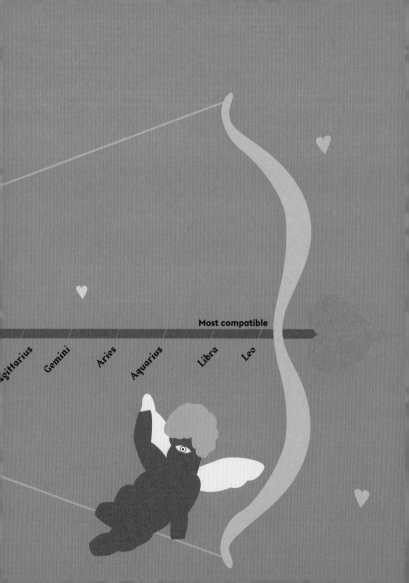

Most compatible

ngittarius   Gemini   Aries   Aquarius   Libra   Leo

The Sagitta

II.

us

Deep Dive

In this section, dive deeper into the ways in which your Sun sign might be driving you or holding you back, and start to think about how you might use this knowledge to inform your path.

The
Sagittarius
home

It might be expected for a sign not much bothered about staying at home, that Sagittarius has little interest in it. But this wouldn't be true because although home is somewhere about which they're probably not particularly sentimental, its existence is important. It probably houses lots of artefacts from far-flung travel trips and a bookshelf full of travel guides, plus there may be friends sleeping on the sofa, because for Sagittarius very often *mi casa es su casa* (my home is your home), there's always a welcome on the mat and every stranger is a friend you haven't yet met. Get the picture?

Sagittarius' style is relaxed, informal and generous. They're not fussy about their possessions and won't invest in high-end luxury because, what's the point? Also, if they're away a lot then house sitters or lodgers will use their stuff. But while it may be a bit scruffy, a Sagittarius home is likely to be very accommodating, with large, comfy sofas and plenty of cushions, and a big kitchen table around which to sit and socialise, long into the night. And the colours might reflect a turquoise Santa Fe sky, the sun-baked terracotta of Mexico, or the shifting sands of the Kalahari, at least in their travel-inspired imagination.

TOP TIPS FOR SAGITTARIUS SELF-CARE

★ Have a duvet day once in a while and catch up on sleep.

★ Don't neglect those glutes: regular exercise will tone the butt and support the hips.

★ Keep hydrated, otherwise energy levels can take a nosedive.

Self-care

Looking after themselves is often a bit of an afterthought for Sagittarius. With a tendency to leap before they look and to burn the candle at both ends, there's the chance of both accidents and burnout: even robust energy reserves need replenishing occasionally. Slowing down might not come naturally to Sagittarius, who are busy chasing after those arrows they've fired, but it is one way of looking after themselves. A bit of self-maintenance can also help avoid problems: regular exercise will keep Sagittarius safe in the proverbial saddle long into old age.

Fortunately, Sagittarius is protected by that planet of good fortune, Jupiter, and generally recovers quickly given half the chance. They're unlikely to take the time at home for a long, perfumed soak in the tub, but get a few friends together for a spa day and it's a different story. Sleep isn't usually a problem once they're in bed, but keeping regular hours is tricky, and jet lag can be a problem, so a sleep deficit may need addressing from time to time. Time out, gentle exercise, regular nutritious meals and a decent night's sleep will all pay off, allowing Sagittarius to run wild and free again.

WHAT TO KEEP IN THE SAGITTARIUS PANTRY

* Quinoa – packed with protein and one of the speediest grains to cook.

* Tinned (canned) olives, to snack on, stir into pasta dishes, or add to salads or pizzas.

* Bananas for fast carbs, to add to yoghurt or even freeze in chunks and whizz into smoothies.

Food
and
cooking

Sagittarius isn't always that sure where the kitchen actually is, because taking time out to eat means time wasted: refuelling is often done on the run, and food is usually just a means to an end.

But just occasionally – maybe if they want to impress a date – Sagittarius will cook. Then there might be some thought and planning involved. Otherwise, it's more often a question of fast food, so anything that can be rustled up in 10 minutes works for them. They seldom think far enough ahead to even put a potato in the oven to bake ... unless they have a microwave, of course. Smart Sagittarius learns how to create fast meals that are nutritous too, though, whether that's adding nuts and seeds to a salad, flash-frying a minute steak, or grilling some salmon.

TOP TIPS FOR SAGITTARIUS' MONEY

* However lucky, don't rely on it and try to live roughly within your means.

* Bills still need to be paid so put money aside for those.

* Speculate, but make sure any risks taken are actually sound.

How Sagittarius handles money

Easy come, easy go, could sum up the way Sagittarius handles money and there's a certain truth in that, illustrated in the way their confident, buoyant nature manages to swan along from one good money-making opportunity to another. Money represents a means to an end for many Sagittarians. They're not particularly attached to it, feel no need to hoard it, and as long as they have enough to do what they want, then that's what it's there for – whether travelling first class or on a shoestring, down the road or across the globe.

There's an easy relationship between sensing opportunities and being prepared to take risks, while not being duly concerned when not everything works out, largely because most things do: win some, lose some, could be another motto for Sagittarius. Either way, the next successful adventure could be a financial venture, in their book. Their generous nature also means they're happy to share good fortune, in all its guises, and that can encourage financial success.

How Sagittarius handles the boss

When they switch on the charm, Sagittarius can get away with a lot in the workplace, and this can be a valuable asset. But using their charm to handle their boss isn't, in itself, enough and promises need to be delivered upon sooner or later in order not to become a serious aggravation. Smart Sagittarians know this, and because they are gregarious, they are often good team players, and can actually be quite inspirational in motivating others and getting the work done.

Sagittarius' frankness, however, can be a problem. Sometimes the workplace calls for a level of diplomacy which is not their strongest suit, because if there's any hypocrisy or devious behaviour, Sagittarius can have an alarming habit of calling it out (or, putting their foot in it), which can sometimes destabilise the work force. Saying the wrong thing at the wrong time can drive a boss to exasperation and backfire badly.

Renowned for their ability to see beyond the obvious, Sagittarius has an innovative take on problem-solving and, in the right job, they can make this work well. But they need to learn to harness their ideas to some hard graft. Then they make seriously good employees on which a boss is happy to rely.

TOP TIPS TO
HANDLE THE BOSS

* Before presenting a new plan to the boss, check it meets the brief.

* Press pause occasionally to check in with the boss – and any team mates.

* Use a task reminder to avoid missing important deadlines.

TOP TIPS FOR AN EASIER LIFE

★ To keep the peace, agree to a rota for household chores – and stick to it.

★ Spontaneous social events work best; too long in the planning will bore you.

★ Let your housemates know that a straightforward request for time or attention works best.

What is Sagittarius like to live with?

On one level, Sagittarius is easy and actually loves to live communally. But they also often choose to spend quite a lot of time away from home, travelling for work, for example.

This is all well and good unless housemates or partners want a little more commitment, whether that is Sagittarius doing their share of the communal chores or showing up for their children's bedtimes. The upside of Sagittarius's unpredictability is that their usually sunny disposition makes them great company, and the minute the sun's up, they'll be on the lookout to make the best use of the day – inviting everyone along for the ride.

Any sort of living arrangement with Sagittarius involves a fair amount of compromise, and the trick is to find which sort of compromise they are willing to make. Attempts to subtly bring Sagittarius to heel often fail but what is easy with Sagittarius is open discussion. It may drive a partner or housemate mad to have to constantly ask for things to be done, but it is usually the only way, as Sagittarius is likely to be oblivious to putting the rubbish out, unless asked to do it.

How to handle a break-up

Sagittarius may think it's OK to gallop off into the sunset with just a metaphorical flick of the tail in farewell when they break up with a lover, but this is often done in defence, irrespective of whether they are the one leaving or being left. And while this fits well with a reputation Sagittarius has for being footloose and fancy free, it can speak volumes about how they deal with heartache: by ignoring it. Given that each relationship is the opportunity for a new adventure, though, they are pretty resilient and will soon be looking for pastures new, although that's not to say they don't care. What they do expect, however, is to be able to stay friends, and in this they are straightforward – and surprised if their ex doesn't feel the same.

TOP TIPS FOR AN EASIER BREAK-UP

★ In being straightforward, don't be too frank about the reasons for breaking up.

★ Remember it takes a little time to process feelings before moving on.

★ Always allow an ex time to recover before trying to become friends.

How Sagittarius wants to be loved

Open-hearted almost to a fault, with a huge capacity for adventure (and an occasional tendency to bolt), Sagittarius appears to think that everyone else is just like them. Consequently, they tend to send mixed messages and it can take a while to work out how they want to be loved – which they do, there's no doubt about that. Sagittarius also expects love to be somewhat elusive, something in the distance found after an adventure or journey along an unexplored path. And they expect to chase and be chased – after all, that's half the fun of love, isn't it? But while the chase is pretty important, it's a chase that leads to a conclusion, right? That's the problematic bit: Sagittarius isn't always so sure.

Sagittarius also wants to be loved for their mind as much as anything else. They really value having someone to share and discuss things with. In fact, being loved as a friend can be the first step to getting close to Sagittarius, although if this is anything other than genuine, they'll know. Using friendship as a deliberate ploy to hook a Sagittarius will probably not work as they have an instinct for bullshit, but solid companionship is important. Sagittarius isn't much of a game player, either, and probably won't try to manipulate a situation by playing hard to get, except – who says you can't flirt with your friends? They just don't seem to take love very seriously, which can be infuriating for a prospective lover or life partner. But it's not really a game to them, it's just how they are, which can all get a little confusing (even to themselves).

Just like everyone else, however, Sagittarius needs to feel loved and secure about it, even if they don't always show it. And, in fact, their independent streak may sometimes be something of an unconscious defence against being disappointed or hurt. It's not that they want to be tamed, they don't, but a secure place to lay their head actually appeals as much as wide-open spaces. These apparent contradictions are easier to understand if you think of the psychological metaphor of their personality, the horse. Loving Sagittarius can be deeply rewarding if you share their yearning for travel and adventure, whether in body or mind.

TOP TIPS FOR
LOVING SAGITTARIUS

* Give them plenty of emotional
  room – that Sagittarius lover
  needs open spaces.

* Mental exploration and good
  conversation are also important.

* Spontaneity is key: routine
  can be the kiss of death to
  this relationship.

Sagittarius' sex life

There's a playfulness about Sagittarius' approach to life that extends into the bedroom. Sex is another form of communication, as far as they're concerned, and like any good conversation it can vary – short and to the point, long and languid, flirty, exploratory, intense, fun – but seldom taken too seriously. Sagittarius very often sees sex in such a straightforward way, they can rather miss the point of its emotional connection as they are already thinking about the next big idea, plan or adventure. All of which can give this sign something of a reputation for fickleness.

Sagittarius has a lot of sexual energy, but at heart is quite relaxed. They're not going to fuss too much unless it's a big romantic event like an engagement or anniversary – there's always going to be another time, either with the one they're with, or with someone else. What's for sure is that they are so cheerful, thoughtful and easy to be with, that as long as they don't get asked for more than they can offer emotionally, Sagittarius generally makes a great lover.

Give

III.

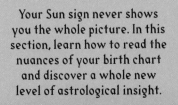

Me More

Your Sun sign never shows you the whole picture. In this section, learn how to read the nuances of your birth chart and discover a whole new level of astrological insight.

Your birth chart

Your birth chart is a snapshot of a particular moment, in a particular place, at the precise moment of your birth and is therefore completely individual to you. It's like a blueprint, a map, a statement of occurrence, spelling out possible traits and influences – but it isn't your destiny. It is just a symbolic tool to which you can refer, based on the position of the planets at the time of your birth. If you can't get to an astrologer, these days anyone can get their birth chart prepared in minutes online (see page 108 for a list of websites and apps that will do it for you). Even if you don't know your exact time of birth, just knowing the date and place of birth can create the beginnings of a useful template.

Remember, nothing is intrinsically good or bad in astrology and there is no explicit timing or forecasting: it's more a question of influences and how these might play out positively or negatively. And if we have some insight, and some tools with which to approach, see or interpret our circumstances and surroundings, this gives us something to work with.

When you are reading your birth chart, it's useful to first understand all the tools of astrology available to you; not only the astrological signs and what they represent, but also the 10 planets referred to in astrology and their individual characteristics, along with the 12 houses and what they mean. Individually, these tools of astrology are of passing interest, but when you start to see how they might sit in juxtaposition to each other, then the bigger picture becomes more accessible and we begin to gain insights that can be useful to us.

Broadly speaking, each of the planets suggests a different type of energy, the astrological signs propose the various ways in which that energy might be expressed, while the houses represent areas of experience in which this expression might operate.

Next to bring into the picture are the positions of the signs at four key points: the ascendant, or rising sign, and its opposite, the descendant; and the midheaven and its opposite, the IC, not to mention the different aspects created by congregations of signs and planets.

It is now possible to see how subtle the reading of a birth chart might be and how it is infinite in its variety, and highly specific to an individual. With this information, and a working understanding of the symbolic meaning and influences of the signs, planets and houses of your unique astrological profile, you can begin to use these tools to help with decision-making and other aspects of life.

Reading your chart

If you have your birth chart prepared, either by hand or via an online program, you will see a circle divided into 12 segments, with information clustered at various points indicating the position of each zodiac sign, in which segment it appears and at what degree. Irrespective of the features that are relevant to the individual, each chart follows the same pattern when it comes to interpretation.

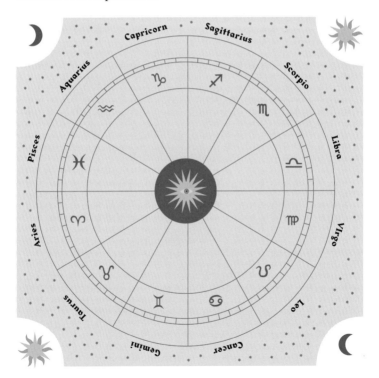

Given the time of birth, the place of birth and the position of the planets at that moment, the birth chart, sometimes called a natal horoscope, is drawn up.

If you consider the chart as a clock face, the first house (see pages 95–99 for the astrological houses) begins at the 9, and it is from this point that, travelling anti-clockwise the chart is read from the first house, through the 12 segments of the chart to the twelfth.

The beginning point, the 9, is also the point at which the Sun rises on your life, giving you your ascendant, or rising sign, and opposite to this, at the 3 of the clock face, is your descendant sign. The midheaven point of your chart, the MC, is at 12, and its opposite, the IC, at 6 (see pages 101–102).

Understanding the significance of the characteristics of the astrological signs and the planets, their particular energies, their placements and their aspects to each other can be helpful in understanding ourselves and our relationships with others. In day-to-day life, too, the changing configuration of planets and their effects are much more easily understood with a basic knowledge of astrology, as are the recurring patterns that can sometimes strengthen and sometimes delay opportunities and possibilities. Working with, rather than against, these trends can make life more manageable and, in the last resort, more successful.

The Moon effect

If your Sun sign represents your consciousness, your life force and your individual will, then the Moon represents that side of your personality that you tend to keep rather secret or hidden. This is the realm of instinct, intuition, creativity and the unconscious, which can take you places emotionally that are sometimes hard to understand. This is what brings great subtlety and nuance to a person, way beyond just their Sun sign. So you may have your Sun in Sagittarius, and all that means, but this might be countered by a strongly empathetic and feeling Moon in Cancer; or you may have your Sun in open-hearted Leo, but a Moon in Aquarius with all its rebellious, emotional detachment.

Phases of the Moon

The Moon orbits the Earth, taking roughly 28 days to do so. How much of the Moon we see is determined by how much of the Sun's light it reflects, giving us the impression that it waxes, or grows, and wanes. When the Moon is new, to us, only a sliver of it is illuminated. As it waxes, it reflects more light and moves from a crescent, to a waxing crescent to a first quarter; then it moves to a waxing gibbous Moon, to a full Moon. Then the Moon begins to wane through a waning gibbous, to a last quarter, and then the cycle begins again. All of this occurs over four weeks. When we have two full Moons in any one calendar month, the second is called a blue Moon.

Each month the Moon also moves through an astrological sign, as we know from our personal birth charts. This, too, will yield information – a Moon in Scorpio can have a very different effect to one in Capricorn – and depending on our personal charts, this can have a shifting influence each month. For example, if the Moon in your birth chart is in Virgo, then when the actual Moon moves into Virgo, this will have an additional influence. Read the characteristics of the signs for further information (see pages 12–17).

The Moon's cycle has an energetic effect, which we can see quite easily on the ocean tides. Astrologically, because the Moon is both a fertility symbol and attuned to our deeper psychological side, we can use this to focus more profoundly and creatively on aspects of life that are important to us.

Eclipses

Generally speaking, an eclipse covers up and prevents light being shed on a situation. Astrologically speaking, this will depend on where the Sun or Moon is positioned in relation to other planets at the time of an eclipse. So if a solar eclipse is in Gemini, there will be a Geminian influence or an influence on Geminis.

Hiding, or shedding, light on an area of our lives is an invitation to pay attention to it. Eclipses are generally about beginnings or endings, which is why our ancestors saw them as portents, important signs to be taken notice of. As it is possible to know when an eclipse is forthcoming, these are charted astronomically; consequently, their astrological significance can be assessed and acted upon ahead of time.

The 10 planets

For the purpose of astrology (but not for astronomy, because the Sun is really a star) we talk about 10 planets, and each astrological sign has a ruling planet, with Mercury, Venus and Mars each being assigned two. The characteristics of each planet describe those influences that can affect signs, all of which information feeds into the interpretation of a birth chart.

The Moon

This sign is an opposing principle to the Sun, forming a pair, and it represents the feminine, symbolising containment and receptivity, how we react most instinctively and with feeling.

Rules the sign of Cancer.

The Sun

The Sun represents the masculine, and is seen as the energy that sparks life, which suggests a paternal energy in our birth chart. It also symbolises our self or essential being, and our purpose.

Rules the sign of Leo.

Mercury

Mercury is the planet of communication and symbolises our urge to make sense of, understand and communicate our thoughts through words.

Rules the signs of Gemini and Virgo.

Venus

The planet of love is all about attraction, connection and pleasure and in a female chart it symbolises her style of femininity, while in a male chart it represents his ideal partner.

Rules the signs of Taurus and Libra.

Mars

This planet symbolises pure energy (Mars was, after all, the god of War) but it also tells you in which areas you're most likely to be assertive, aggressive or to take risks.

Rules the signs of Aries and Scorpio.

Saturn

Saturn is sometimes called the wise teacher or taskmaster of astrology, symbolising lessons learnt and limitations, showing us the value of determination, tenacity and resilience.

Rules the sign of Capricorn.

Jupiter

The planet Jupiter is the largest in our solar system and symbolises bounty and benevolence, all that is expansive and jovial. Like the sign it rules, it's also about moving away from the home on journeys and exploration.

Rules the sign of Sagittarius.

Uranus

This planet symbolises the unexpected, new ideas and innovation, and the urge to tear down the old and usher in the new. The downside can mark an inability to fit in and consequently the feeling of being an outsider.

Rules the sign of Aquarius.

Pluto

Aligned to Hades (*Pluto* in Latin), the god of the underworld or death, this planet exerts a powerful force that lies below the surface and which, in its most negative form, can represent obsessions and compulsive behaviour.

Rules the sign of Scorpio.

Neptune

Linked to the sea, this is about what lies beneath, underwater and too deep to be seen clearly. Sensitive, intuitive and artistic, it also symbolises the capacity to love unconditionally, to forgive and forget.

Rules the sign of Pisces.

The four elements

Further divisions of the 12 astrological signs into the four elements of earth, fire, air and water yield other characteristics. This comes from ancient Greek medicine, where the body was considered to be made up of four bodily fluids or 'humours'. These four humours – blood, yellow bile, black bile and phlegm – corresponded to the four temperaments of sanguine, choleric, melancholic and phlegmatic, to the four seasons of the year, spring, summer, autumn, winter, and the four elements of air, fire, earth and water.

Related to astrology, these symbolic qualities cast further light on characteristics of the different signs. Carl Jung also used them in his psychology, and we still refer to people as earthy, fiery, airy or wet in their approach to life, while sometimes describing people as 'being in their element'. In astrology, those Sun signs that share the same element are said to have an affinity, or an understanding, with each other.

Like all aspects of astrology, there is always a positive and a negative, and a knowledge of any 'shadow side' can be helpful in terms of self-knowledge and what we may need to enhance or balance out, particularly in our dealings with others.

Air

GEMINI ✶ LIBRA ✶ AQUARIUS

The realm of ideas is where these air signs excel. Perceptive and visionary and able to see the big picture, there is a very reflective quality to air signs that helps to vent situations. Too much air, however, can dissipate intentions, so Gemini might be indecisive, Libra has a tendency to sit on the fence, while Aquarius can be very disengaged.

Fire

ARIES ✶ LEO ✶ SAGITTARIUS

There is a warmth and energy to these signs, a positive approach, spontaneity and enthusiasm that can be inspiring and very motivational to others. The downside is that Aries has a tendency to rush in headfirst, Leo can have a need for attention and Sagittarius can tend to talk it up but not deliver.

Earth

TAURUS ✴ VIRGO ✴ CAPRICORN

Characteristically, these signs enjoy sensual pleasure, relishing food and other physical satisfactions, and they like to feel grounded, preferring to base their ideas in facts. The downside is that Taureans can be stubborn, Virgos can be pernickety and Capricorns can veer towards a dogged conservatism.

Water

CANCER ✴ SCORPIO ✴ PISCES

Water signs are very responsive, like the tide ebbing and flowing, and can be very perceptive and intuitive, sometimes uncannily so because of their ability to feel. The downside is – watery enough – a tendency to feel swamped, and then Cancer can be both tenacious and self-protective, Pisces chameleon-like in their attention and Scorpio unpredictable and intense.

Cardinal, fixed and mutable signs

In addition to the 12 signs being divided into four elements, they can also be grouped into three different ways in which their energies may act or react, giving further depth to each sign's particular characteristics.

Cardinal

ARIES ✳ CANCER ✳ LIBRA ✳ CAPRICORN

These are action planets, with an energy that takes the initiative and gets things started. Aries has the vision, Cancer the feelings, Libra the contacts and Capricorn the strategy.

Fixed

TAURUS ✳ LEO ✳ SCORPIO ✳ AQUARIUS

Slower but more determined, these signs work to progress and maintain those initiatives that the cardinal signs have fired up. Taurus offers physical comfort, Leo loyalty, Scorpio emotional support and Aquarius sound advice. You can count on fixed signs, but they tend to resist change.

Mutable

GEMINI ✳ VIRGO ✳ SAGITTARIUS ✳ PISCES

Adaptable and responsive to new ideas, places and people, mutable signs have a unique ability to adjust to their surroundings. Gemini is mentally agile, Virgo is practical and versatile, Sagittarius visualises possibilities and Pisces is responsive to change.

The 12 houses

The birth chart is divided into 12 houses, which represent separate areas and functions of your life. When you are told you have something in a specific house – for example, Libra (balance) in the fifth house (creativity and sex) – it creates a way of interpreting the influences that can arise and are particular to how you might approach an aspect of your life.

Each house relates to a Sun sign, and in this way each is represented by some of the characteristics of that sign, which is said to be its natural ruler.

Three of these houses are considered to be mystical, relating to our interior, psychic world: the fourth (home), eighth (death and regeneration) and twelfth (secrets).

1st House

THE SELF

RULED BY ARIES

This house symbolises the self: you, who you are and how you represent yourself, your likes, dislikes and approach to life. It also represents how you see yourself and what you want in life.

2nd House

POSSESSIONS

RULED BY TAURUS

The second house symbolises your possessions, what you own, including money; how you earn or acquire your income; and your material security and the physical things you take with you as you move through life.

3rd House

COMMUNICATION

RULED BY GEMINI

This house is about communication and mental attitude, primarily how you express yourself. It's also about how you function within your family, and how you travel to school or work, and includes how you think, speak, write and learn.

4ᵗʰ **House**

HOME

RULED BY CANCER

This house is about your roots and
your home or homes, present, past
and future, so it includes both your
childhood and current domestic
set-up. It's also about what home
and security represents to you.

5ᵗʰ **House**

CREATIVITY

RULED BY LEO

Billed as the house of creativity
and play, this also includes sex,
and relates to the creative urge,
the libido, in all its manifestations.
It's also about speculation in
finance and love, games, fun and
affection: affairs of the heart.

6ᵗʰ **House**

HEALTH

RULED BY VIRGO

This house is related to health: our
own physical and emotional health,
and how robust it is; but also those
we care for, look after or provide
support to – from family members
to work colleagues.

7th **House**

PARTNERSHIPS

RULED BY LIBRA

The opposite of the first house, this reflects shared goals and intimate partnerships, our choice of life partner and how successful our relationships might be. It also reflects partnerships and adversaries in our professional world.

8th **House**

REGENERATION

RULED BY SCORPIO

For death, read regeneration or spiritual transformation: this house also reflects legacies and what you inherit after death, in personality traits or materially. And because regeneration requires sex, it's also about sex and sexual emotions.

9th **House**

TRAVEL

RULED BY SAGITTARIUS

The house of long-distance travel and exploration, this is also about the broadening of the mind that travel can bring, and how that might express itself. It also reflects the sending out of ideas, which can come about from literary effort or publication.

11th House

FRIENDSHIPS

RULED BY AQUARIUS

The eleventh house is about friendship groups and acquaintances, vision and ideas, and is less about immediate gratification but more concerning longer-term dreams and how these might be realised through our ability to work harmoniously with others.

12th House

SECRETS

RULED BY PISCES

Considered the most spiritual house, it is also the house of the unconscious, of secrets and of what might lie hidden, the metaphorical skeleton in the closet. It also reflects the secret ways we might self-sabotage or imprison our own efforts by not exploring them.

10th House

ASPIRATIONS

RULED BY CAPRICORN

This represents our aspiration and status, how we'd like to be elevated in public standing (or not), our ambitions, image and what we'd like to attain in life, through our own efforts.

The ascendant

Otherwise known as your rising sign, this is the sign of the zodiac that appears at the horizon as dawn breaks on the day of your birth, depending on your location in the world and time of birth. This is why knowing your time of birth is a useful factor in astrology, because your 'rising sign' yields a lot of information about those aspects of your character that are more on show, how you present yourself and how you are seen by others.

So, even if you are a Sun Sagittarius, but have Cancer rising, you may be seen as someone who is maternal, with a noticeable commitment to the domestic life in one way or another. Knowing your own ascendant – or that of another person – will often help explain why there doesn't seem to be such a direct correlation between their personality and their Sun sign.

As long as you know your time of birth and where you were born, working out your ascendant using an online tool or app is very easy (see page 108). Just ask your mum or other family members, or check your birth certificate (in those countries that include a birth time). If the astrological chart were a clock face, the ascendant would be at the 9 o'clock position.

The descendant

The descendant gives an indication of a possible life partner, based on the idea that opposites attract. Once you know your ascendant, the descendant is easy to work out as it is always six signs away: for example, if your ascendant is Virgo, your descendant is Pisces. If the astrological chart were a clock face, the descendant would be at the 3 o'clock position.

The midheaven (MC)

Also included in the birth chart is the position of the midheaven or MC (from the Latin, *medium coeli*, meaning middle of the heavens), which indicates your attitude towards your work, career and professional standing. If the astrological chart were a clock face, the MC would be at the 12 o'clock position.

The IC

Finally, your IC (from the Latin, *imum coeli*, meaning the lowest part of the heavens) indicates your attitude towards your home and family, and is also related to the end of your life. Your IC will be directly opposite your MC: for example, if your MC is Aquarius, your IC is Leo. If the astrological chart were a clock face, the IC would be at the 6 o'clock position.

Saturn return

Saturn is one of the slower-moving planets, taking around 28 years to complete its orbit around the Sun and return to the place it occupied at the time of your birth. This return can last between two to three years and be very noticeable in the period coming up to our thirtieth and sixtieth birthdays, often considered to be significant 'milestone' birthdays.

Because the energy of Saturn is sometimes experienced as demanding, this isn't always an easy period of life. A wise teacher or a hard taskmaster, some consider the Saturn effect as 'cruel to be kind' in the way that many good teachers can be, keeping us on track like a rigorous personal trainer.

Everyone experiences their Saturn return relevant to their circumstances, but it is a good time to take stock, let go of the stuff in your life that no longer serves you and revise your expectations, while being unapologetic about what you would like to include more of in your life. So if you are experiencing or anticipating this life event, embrace and work with it because what you learn now – about yourself, mainly – is worth knowing, however turbulent it might be, and can pay dividends in how you manage the next 28 years!

Mercury
retrograde

Even those with little interest in astrology often take notice when the planet Mercury is retrograde. Astrologically, retrogrades are periods when planets are stationary but, as we continue to move forwards, Mercury 'appears' to move backwards. There is a shadow period either side of a retrograde period, when it could be said to be slowing down or speeding up, which can also be a little turbulent. Generally speaking, the advice is not to make any important moves related to communication on a retrograde and, even if a decision is made, know that it's likely to change.

Given that Mercury is the planet of communication, you can immediately see why there are concerns about its retrograde status and its link to communication failures – of the old-fashioned sort when the post office loses a letter, or the more modern technological variety when your computer crashes

– causing problems. Mercury retrograde can also affect travel, with delays in flights or train times, traffic jams or collisions. Mercury also influences personal communications: listening, speaking, being heard (or not), and can cause confusion or arguments. It can also affect more formal agreements, like contracts between buyer and seller.

These retrograde periods occur three to four times a year, lasting for roughly three weeks, with a shadow period either side. The dates in which it happens also mean it occurs within a specific astrological sign. If, for example, it occurs between 25 October and 15 November, its effect would be linked to the characteristics of Scorpio. In addition, those Sun sign Scorpios, or those with Scorpio in significant placements in their chart, may also experience a greater effect.

Mercury retrograde dates are easy to find from an astrological table, or ephemeris, and online. These can be used in order to avoid planning events that might be affected around these times. How Mercury retrograde may affect you more personally requires knowledge of your birth chart and an understanding of its more specific combination of influences with the signs and planets in your chart.

If you are going to weather a Mercury retrograde more easily, be aware that glitches can occur so, to some extent, expect delays and double-check details. Stay positive if postponements occur and consider this period an opportunity to slow down, review or reconsider ideas in your business or your personal life. Use the time to correct mistakes or reshape plans, preparing for when any stuck energy can shift and you can move forward again more smoothly.

Further reading

Astrology Decoded (2013) by Sue Merlyn Farebrother; published by Rider

Astrology for Dummies (2007) by Rae Orion; published by Wiley Publishing

Chart Interpretation Handbook: Guidelines for Understanding the Essentials of the Birth Chart (1990) by Stephen Arroyo; published by CRCS Publications

Jung's Studies in Astrology (2018) by Liz Greene; published by RKP

The Only Astrology Book You'll Ever Need (2012) by Joanne Woolfolk; published by Taylor Trade

Websites

astro.com

astrologyzone.com

jessicaadams.com

shelleyvonstrunkel.com

Apps

Astrostyle

Co-Star

Susan Miller's Astrology Zone

The Daily Horoscope

The Pattern

Time Passages

Acknowledgements

Particular thanks are due to my trusty team of Taureans. Firstly, to Kate Pollard, Publishing Director at Hardie Grant, for her passion for beautiful books and for commissioning this series. And to Bex Fitzsimons for all her good natured and conscientious editing. And finally to Evi O. Studio, whose illustration and design talents have produced small works of art. With such a star-studded team, these books can only shine and for that, my thanks.

About the author

Stella Andromeda has been studying
astrology for over 30 years, believing that
a knowledge of the constellations of the
skies and their potential for psychological
interpretation can be a useful tool. This
extension of her study into book form makes
modern insights about the ancient wisdom
of the stars easily accessible, sharing her
passion that reflection and self-knowledge
only empowers us in life. With her sun in
Taurus, Aquarius ascendant and Moon
in Cancer, she utilises earth, air and water
to inspire her own astrological journey.

Published in 2019 by Hardie Grant Books,
an imprint of Hardie Grant Publishing

Hardie Grant Books (London)
5th & 6th Floors
52–54 Southwark Street
London, SE1 1UN

Hardie Grant Books (Melbourne)
Building I, 658 Church Street
Richmond, Victoria 3121

hardiegrantbooks.com

British Library Cataloguing-in-Publication Data. A catalogue record
for this book is available from the British Library.

Sagittarius
ISBN: 9781784882693

10 9 8 7 6 5

Publishing Director: Kate Pollard
Junior Editor: Bex Fitzsimons
Art Direction and Illustrations: Evi O. Studio
Editor: Wendy Hobson
Production Controller: Sinead Hering

Colour reproduction by p2d
Printed and bound in China by Leo Paper Products Ltd.